IN PURSUIT *of* LIFE

The Ultimate Guide For Finding Living Kidney Donors

RISA SIMON

In Pursuit of a Better Life:
The Ultimate Guide for Finding Living Kidney Donors

FIRST EDITION
First release January 2017 (Enhanced October 2018)

Disclaimer: This book is *not* intended to replace medical advice or recommendations by healthcare providers. If you are dealing with a medical concern, seek medical attention from a competent provider immediately.

Copyright© 2018 TransplantFirst Academy

Printed in the United States of America

ISBN-13: 9781539731726
ISBN-10: 1539731723

TRANSPLANTFIRST
EMPOWERED PATIENT ACADEMY

The TransplantFirst Academy (TFA) is a 501c3 non-profit corporation that exists to ensure all kidney patients are given an opportunity to proactively pursue a preemptive path to a (live-donor) transplant *before* they approach the need for dialysis.

TFA educates all transplant candidates, including transplant-eligible dialysis patients, on living kidney donor outreach campaigns and communication strategies that offer a faster track to transplant.

TFA passionately advocates for initiatives that protect and recognize living kidney donors for their remarkable humanitarianism, which saves and improves lives—and inspires ordinary people to seek extraordinary acts of human kindness.

This book is dedicated to **you** for daring to explore proactive pathways to a better life.

PREFACE

My greatest fear had suddenly become a chilling reality when tests confirmed I inherited the same kidney disease that took my father's life in his early forties and my grandmother's life before I was born. I felt kidnapped by my own genetics and doomed by its legacy.

I prayed my life would be different. The realism of someday having countless cysts overtake my kidneys rattled my core. My nephrologist told me to relax. He said I was ahead of the eight ball with premature concerns. Evidently, I wasn't sick enough to further the conversation. The notion of becoming *sick enough* haunted me.

While it didn't happen all at once, my kidney function continued to decline at a frightening pace. Desperate for guidance, I jumped on a plane to attend a kidney patient conference. The priceless pearls of information I gleaned catapulted me on to a game-changing track. I found myself back in the driver's seat of life, resetting my navigation system towards a more promising destination.

My mind was reeling the entire flight home. From my thirty-five-thousand-foot view, I debunked all that *"wait until you are sicker"* gibberish. I was on a new mission to secure a better future by becoming my own best advocate.

By the time the cabin door aligned with the gate, I felt an incredible sense of renewal. I knew I was on to something big. I snatched my bags and hit the ground running in search of my best life possible.

I became an inquiring mind on a laser focused expedition. I searched the internet, interviewed medical professionals and polled those who had walked this path before me. The more I learned, the more I realized how much I didn't know.

I discovered astonishing benefits in choosing a transplant over dialysis. I also learned it was best to avoid dialysis before receiving a transplant. I was stunned that I had been led to believe both dialysis and transplant held similar value.

Short of being educated on their respective procedures, transplant wasn't being touted as the best option. Later I learned this philosophy was adopted to avoid disheartening patients who couldn't meet transplant eligibility criteria. *But what does that say for those who could?*

Although I didn't require renal replacement at the time, I knew the day was approaching. I burrowed my way through a maze of choices and discovered the magic kingdom of *preemptive transplantation*—a transplant secured before the need for dialysis.

Assessing the nation's organ shortage and its dreadful wait for a deceased donor's kidney—I became fixated on doing all that I could to find a living kidney donor.

I started talking about our nation's organ crisis with anyone willing to listen. Eventually, I advanced the conversation by weaving my own story into the mix. The response was amazing.

Most listeners wanted to learn more—and nearly two dozen people asked if they could help in some way.

Over time, a handful of interested parties stepped forward to contact my transplant center and set up their evaluations. It felt like the longest 18 months of my life.

One by one, those who tested were subsequently disqualified. Daunted by disappointment, I refused to let unfavorable circumstances hijack my mission. I knew in my heart my ideal donor was out there. I just needed to identify what was keeping us apart.

I was doing all the right things. I shared my story, invited others to share my story, set goals and even wrote intention statements to attract my goals. What was I missing?

And then, like a bolt of lightning, it hit me. I was coming from a place of hopeful *uncertainty,* rather than convicted *belief.* It was time to imagine my dreams as real-time realities.

I rewrote my intention statement *as if* I had already met my ideal kidney donor. I proclaimed all tests had been approved and we were a match. I described our surgeries as being successful and uneventful. I was immensely grateful.

Within ten days my ideal donor appeared.

She was not the typical volunteer for this type of engagement. Not a family member, distant relative or life-long friend. She was a transplant nurse who had witnessed too many unnecessary deaths due to organ donation reluctance.

We were newbie acquaintances. *Kindred-spirits* is how she described it. Coincidentally, the lab tests revealed that the bond we shared went beyond visceral intangibles.

Melissa and I held a four out of six "sister-like" match!

I affectionately nicknamed my newly adopted kidney *MAK*—a most fitting acronym for <u>M</u>elissa's <u>A</u>mazing <u>K</u>idney. Melissa insists the gift she gave was just as much a gift to her *as* it was to me. Never claiming to be a hero, she said she simply did what she felt was the right thing to do.

As for me, I describe it all in one word—Grateful. I'm grateful Melissa chose me. I'm grateful for the gift of *MAK*. I'm grateful for this *extra*ordinary life-changing experience—and I'm grateful I found the courage to proactively seek this amazing life I now live.

Realizing that an opportunity of this magnitude doesn't come often, I ask you "Are you willing to do the necessary work to bring forth a better quality of life for yourself?"

If your answer is an enthusiastic "YES!" then I ask you to embrace this book as an inspirational guide for the journey ahead. As you advance through these pages, recognize your power to walk *before* your diagnosis, as a top contender in one of the most important marathons of your life.

While I don't know your story; there is one thing I do know. Ordinary people can achieve extraordinary results when they give it their *all*.

This book is your "ON" switch. Flip it on, be *"all in"* and expect to be amazed. The best is yet to come!

Risa Simon

Risa Simon, CMC
Founder, TransplantFirst Academy

TABLE OF CONTENTS

Foreword

It was a serendipitous event that led to my first encounter with Risa. She was a patient in our transplant program at Mayo Clinic in Arizona, where I was the Operations Manager responsible for overall management of the abdominal solid organ transplant programs, including the Living Kidney Donor Program—a cause I feel deeply passionate about both personally and professionally.

From the beginning, it was clear that Risa and I had a common interest in "pro-active" management for chronic kidney disease patients and in promoting living kidney donation. Our common interest grew into a shared purpose—and our "thought bubble" grew to read: *We Can Do More!* We agreed there was much work to be done—Risa in her world and me in mine.

Risa and I developed a friendship. We would meet occasionally to discuss CKD patients and life in general. Whenever I talked on too long about transplant-related matters, Risa didn't get a glazed look in her eyes like others would—rather, she responded with matched enthusiasm. I knew I had met one of my people in Risa.

Among the issues we discussed, the gap in information and education for chronic kidney disease patients regarding all available treatment options remained the common headline to our gatherings. We heard from patients that the information they were provided was often unclear, incomplete or missing.

Assumptions were being made by providers on behalf of patients that dialysis would be the treatment plan, rather than giving patients the information and opportunity to explore transplant options. We knew that assumptions like those could adversely alter the course of a CKD patient's life.

We also knew from the data that a certain percentage of CKD patients are not eligible to be transplant candidates. However, it is also true that many CKD patients could write a different end to their story if they were just given the right information at the proper time.

As clinicians, we can educate on clinical details, pathophysiology, side effects of meds and other relevant clinical information about the disease a person has. However, no one's health care team can speak to what it's like to be the patient. That sacred role is reserved for those who have walked a mile in those shoes.

This book is a first of its kind written by someone who has walked that mile. Risa has outlined a heartfelt response to the dilemma you may not have known you were facing. The book before you can be your ticket to freedom—the only missing ingredient is you.

Risa has invested in your future by graciously taking on the role of personal tour guide. There is no better role model or cheerleader for you on this journey than Risa. It is my hope that you will use the information provided to take control of your health so that you can live your best life now.

I had the privilege of witnessing the transformation of the author, Risa, on her journey to freedom—and was even allowed the opportunity to play a role. Not only do Risa and I share the same goal for you—to live your best possible life—we also share one set of kidneys.

That's right. On June 8, 2010, I became a living kidney donor by donating my right kidney to Risa. The surgeries occurred simultaneously.

It was my team of physicians, nurses and technicians who either performed or assisted in this surgical miracle that allowed me to give new life to Risa.

It was an invaluable experience to be both an RN and Operations Administrator on the "other side" of our system. One of the most gratifying experiences in being a living kidney donor has been the opportunity to witness the recipient bounce back metabolically after transplant.

To know that someone's life is improved as a direct result of a decision made by me—there are no words to describe the "feel good" that derives from that.

The opportunity to be a living kidney donor for Risa was *my* privilege. The perspective I now have for what it's like to be a patient calling into our center, to be cared for in my department or checked into our transplant wing—is invaluable.

Meeting Risa was perhaps one of the most fortunate and significant things that ever happened to me. As you meet her in this book, I believe you will find that to be true for yourself as well.

Blessings,

Melissa Blevins Bein

Melissa Blevins Bein, MS, RN

Introduction

You've been waiting months and months—perhaps several years, for a kidney transplant from a deceased donor. The meter's running, the clock's ticking and every day counts. You're either hoping to bypass the need for dialysis *or* praying you'll be off dialysis someday soon.

This is *not* a time to sit back and stop doing. You've been told to ask your family and friends for help, but what exactly do you ask for and how do you go about asking it? You cringe at the thought of having to ask *anything* at all.

You know you're supposed to *share your story*, but that's not as easy as it sounds. This book was written to make this process easier for you and help your story-telling be more engaging for others. It provides insights on how to initiate conversations, create need-awareness and ask for help.

On the pages to follow, you'll find confidence-building communication strategies *and* well-intentioned outreach tactics to help you share your story and increase awareness in your need for a living kidney donor.

Whether you're seeking a transplant before dialysis is required (*known as preemptive transplant*), or you're hoping to eliminate your need for dialysis, you're on the right path to a better life. [1,2,5]

After reading this book, you'll be able to:

1. Share your story to increase need awareness.
2. Build an advocacy team to help you find potential donors.
3. Attract good-hearted people interested in living donation.
4. Increase your chances of getting a transplant.

Understanding the Process

Typically, there are three types of readers attracted to this book. There are those who are seeking to avoid the need for dialysis, those who are already on dialysis and individuals who are concerned about the wellbeing of someone in this space.

Whether this book is for you or someone in need, the goal remains the same—to find a suitable living kidney donor and advance to transplant, rather than waiting years for a kidney from a deceased donor.

While your journey ahead will be full of hope and excitement, it's important to be emotionally prepared for a lack of donor interest and medical disqualifications. Finding a living kidney donor requires an immense amount of time, far more than most imagine. This process also entails a high degree of unpredictability. That said, it's important to stay focused on the reward that awaits you—a better life ahead.

First Things First

All you need to do right now is learn more about living kidney donation, the transplant process and the best way for you to communicate your need. As you learn more, share what you've learned with others. Include your need for a transplant and hope for finding a living kidney donor. Tap into your listeners heartstrings and you're sure to trigger curiosity, introspect and a genuine desire to help.

You can also invite other people to share your story. Your best advocates are those who thought they could donate a kidney— but can't. Basically, anyone who cares about you will want to help in some way. Just ask. You might be pleasantly surprised.

Why Living Donors Offer Better Outcomes

It's important to understand the value of living donor kidneys as compared to deceased donor kidneys. This outline highlights the difference:

1. **Avoid the Wait.** When you have an approved living donor, the surgery date can be scheduled as soon as the donor is available, and the hospital can schedule the surgery.

2. **Give Someone Else Your Place in Line.** Once you have an approved living kidney donor, your name no longer needs to be on the national transplant waitlist. By taking your name off the list, the wait time for others is shortened.

3. **Longer Transplant Success.** A person who receives a kidney transplant from a living donor gains more years of function (also known as graft function), when compared to transplants from a deceased donor's kidney. [3,4]

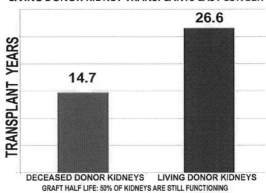

LIVING DONOR KIDNEY TRANSPLANTS LAST LONGER

GRAFT HALF LIFE: 50% OF KIDNEYS ARE STILL FUNCTIONING

SOURCE: 2010 OPTN/SRTR ANNUAL DATA REPORT

4. **Higher Success Rates.** Transplants performed with kidneys from living kidney donors have better outcomes. **Preemptive transplants (transplants performed before the need for dialysis) have the best outcomes.** [5,6,7]

   Living kidney donors offer value to transplant-eligible dialysis patients as well, because a transplant received after dialysis is better than *continued* dialysis. Published medical data has shown that the transplanted kidney will work much longer in patients transplanted before they start dialysis. Patients who wait for a transplant on dialysis for two years are three times more likely to lose their transplanted kidney than those patients who wait less than six months on dialysis. [5]

5. **Bypass Dialysis.** When you're proactively seeking potential living kidney donors *before* you need dialysis, your chances of avoiding dialysis significantly improves.

   The goal is to avoid dialysis completely. However, when this is not possible, the goal is to shorten your long-term need. As an approved candidate, it is in your best interest to make transplant a priority. This will help you avoid health issues that lead to transplant disqualification. [5,8]

6. **Peace of Mind.** Living kidney donors must go through extensive testing to gain approval. Rest assured your donor was medically cleared for their safety and yours.

7. **Immediate Function.** In deceased donation, there is a possibility of delayed graft function (DGF), which is known as having a "sleepy kidney." When this is the case, dialysis is required until the kidney wakes up and starts functioning. This is not common with live-donor kidneys.

8. **Find Your Best Match.** Living donor testing can help you secure a stronger genetic match, which increases the long-term success of the organ.

9. **Donor Exchange Options.** If your donor is medically approved to donate but found to be a mismatch due to blood type incompatibilities or antibodies that could cause rejection, a donor exchange program can be considered. Donor exchange programs allow incompatible donor-recipients to exchange "donor partners," so they can advance to transplants with higher success rates. *Refer to page 13, Kidney Paired Donation (KPD).*

It is quite common to feel overwhelmed as you learn more about living kidney donation. Imagining what it would be like to accept a gift of this magnitude can be equally overwhelming. To that, I offer you a shift in perspective: If your hope is to obtain a quality of life that would allow you to give the "best of yourself" to others; then you must open your heart and allow others to give their "best self" to you. Their "best self" could well be—one of their kidneys!

How to Increase Potential Donor Interest

First, make your friends and family aware of your declining renal function. Start this process by sharing your story with friends and family. Describe the value of receiving a living kidney donor transplant in a natural and factual way. Acknowledge your emotions and speak from the heart.

If you are choosing a transplant over dialysis, tell your friends and family why this is your first choice. Share your story and supporting facts. Use the communication examples and letter samples found (starting on page 48) to help you express your situation and goals in written form.

Your communication style should empathetically draw listeners into your story. Consider using the following talking points to trigger a human connection and ignite story buzz.

Key Talking Points

- [ ] Your need (and sense of urgency) for a kidney transplant
- [ ] Our organ shortage (100,000 in U.S. wait on a list for a kidney)
- [ ] The average wait for a kidney from a deceased donor
- [ ] Living donors eliminate this life-threatening wait
- [ ] The wait often requires dialysis and negative impacts
- [ ] Transplants from living donors are known to last longer
- [ ] Transplants from living donors often perform better
- [ ] Initial screenings are offered by online and by phone

And here's a key talking point to yourself: Stay optimistically open-minded at all times. Asking for help is not a pointless process. Assuming if someone really wanted to help you, they would have offered already—is foolish thinking! Recognize that it's difficult for anyone to imagine how they could help you if they don't know what it is that you need, or how they might be able to fulfill that need. It's up to you to paint that picture while sharing your story.

Story Elements

Your story can be far more engaging when it identities personal elements about you and your goals, such as:

- [ ] Your medical condition and need for a transplant
- [ ] Your blood type, though donors don't have to be a match
- [ ] Your transplant center location and contact information
- [ ] How a donor doesn't have to be blood related
- [ ] How your insurance pays for donor testing and surgery
- [ ] Expense reimbursement (travel and lost wages) options*
- [ ] Your "bucket list" and quality-of-life goals

(For example, your hope might be to see your grandchildren grow up, or you might aspire to pay-it-forward by mentoring other kidney patients after you receive your transplant.)

The key here is to be sure your friends and family understand your needs, so they can imagine all the ways in which they can help you. *(Refer to letter samples starting on page 48.)*

*Financial programs and charities that offer support include, the American Living Organ Donor Fund (ALODF) http://www.ALODF.org, and The National Living Donor Assistance Center: https://www.livingdonorassistance.org.

Casual Conversation Opportunities

Make the most of everyday conversations. You do this by creating a more dynamic response to one of the most commonly asked questions, "How are you?" When someone asks how you're doing, thank them for asking and then start dropping some breadcrumbs about your current situation.

"Thanks so much for asking! I'm hanging in there. I'm still waiting for a kidney transplant—and when I find a person who can be my living donor, my life is going to be amazing!"

Look for an opening to tell your story and wait for listeners to ask questions. As the conversation flows, use your gut to determine how much you should share *or* not. Watch for signs of interest or curiosity. If the listener seems interested, continue sharing more details. When you don't sense interest, allow the conversation to naturally come to an end.

Never underestimate your audience. Some of your least likely prospects can end up being some of your best influencers.

Build a network of individuals willing to advocate on your behalf by spreading the word about your need.

Provide your team of *Donor Outreach Advocates* additional talking points. When you provide expanded talking points, your *Donor Outreach Advocates* will be able to describe your story, explain your goals and comfortably engage listeners.

Additional talking points can include:

☐ What caused your kidneys to fail?

☐ Why a transplant would offer you the best outcome.

☐ Your hope of finding a living donor *before* requiring dialysis.

☐ If already on dialysis, your hope to become dialysis-free.

☐ How long you've been waiting and associated risks.

☐ How incompatible blood types *can still* donate (KPD, pg. 13)

☐ How interested parties can call your center to learn more.

☐ How your transplant center's success is rated. *

*To find and compare transplant center programs, visit:
http://www.srtr.org/about-the-data/comparing-transplant-programs/)

Work from a script. Develop a script and practice so the telling of your story becomes second nature, and facts flow logically and remain consistent.

While this is important for your story sharing, it's especially important for your *Donor Outreach Team,* who is less familiar with your story. Scripts should be written and rehearsed until the content is easy to communicate *without* reading.

Avoid direct "ASKs." When your message is a direct "ask," it can pressure listeners to jump to awkward and disingenuous responses. Potential donors are evaluated to ensure they are donating for the right reasons, though it is best to get that settled before you refer them to your transplant center.

When your transplant center suspects pressure or coercion, disqualification will follow. For this reason, stay mindful of your conversations.

Increase awareness and create goodwill BUZZ for *all* those in need. Keep your focus on the "collaborative good" and good intentions will find their way back to you.

Donor Qualification Snapshot

There are several factors that go into evaluating living kidney donor eligibility. While donors must be at least 18 years of age, they must also be in good physical and mental health.

For example, living kidney donors **must be free of active disease, infections** or conditions that could put them at risk.

Active **disease, infections** or conditions may include:

- Active Infections like Hepatitis C, HIV

- Cancer

- Uncontrolled high blood pressure

- Heart disease

- Liver disease

- Lung disease

- Obesity

- Pregnancy

- Mental Instability

Remember, living donors need to step forward as *volunteers*. If there is suspicion of pressure, guilt or coercion (at any time during the evaluation process), testing will be discontinued, and the donor will be disqualified.

Don't Ask, Tell!

The good news here is that you should never have to "ask" anyone to consider being your donor. If you're asking for anything, you're asking for help in "spreading the word" about your need. **All you need to do is share your story as often as you can *and* with as many people as you can.**

Start by sharing your story to increase awareness for *all* those in need. This makes the process a bit less awkward when it's not just about you. Feeling awkward is very common, so don't sweat it. With each telling it *will* get easier and you *will* get better.

As you tell your story, separate yourself from your disease. **You are not your disease. You are a human being who has a kidney disease diagnosis.**

The more often you share your story, the greater your chance of gaining interest and offers from potential donors.

Some of your offers may come from individuals with compatible blood types, and some from incompatible blood types. The good news is that incompatible blood types don't disqualify donation. There's a workaround for those who are healthy enough to donate, regardless of their blood type.

Understanding Donor Compatibility & Kidney Paired Donation (KPD)

Approximately one-third of interested donors are ruled out because they are blood-type incompatible or have antibody challenges that could cause organ rejection.

Compatibility is based on three factors, <u>Blood-Type Matching</u>, <u>Human Leukocyte Antigens</u> and <u>Immune System Antibodies</u>.

Factor #1: Blood-Type Matching

Recipient w/blood type A = Needs blood type of A *or* O donors
Recipient w/blood type B = Needs blood type of B *or* O donors
Recipient w/blood type AB = Needs A *or* B *or* AB *or* O donors
Recipient w/blood type O = Can only receive from blood type O

*Note: Many transplant centers subtype blood type A and AB donors as A1a, A1b, A2 or A2B. An A2 or A2B donor is referred to as A1-negative, A or non-A1. Oftentimes blood type A and non-A1 donors **can give to blood type O or B candidates**. Likewise, "AB, non-A1B" donors can often give to blood group B candidates. *optn.transplant.hrsa.gov/resources/guidance*

Factor #2: Human Leukocyte Antigen (Histocompatibility), known as HLA.

Your HLA is a specific genetic marker located on the surface of your white blood cells. There are several groups of HLA and many different specific HLA proteins.

There are six markers closely evaluated, three inherited from your mother and three from your father. The goal in cross-matching is to match a high number of antigens with your donor. *Immunosuppressant drugs have made matching far less important, though it still supports long-term graft outcomes.*

Factor #3: Immune System Antibodies.

While antibodies are normally considered good to ward off infection and disease, as a transplant patient your immune system's ability to produce antibodies to fight against (or reject) your donor's kidney is <u>not</u> a good thing.

You can ask your transplant center for an antibody level score. This can be found from your ***Panel Reactive Antibody*** (PRA) test. The way in which your antibodies respond to potential donors is of key importance.

To determine potential problems, the lab mixes a small amount of your blood with an equal amount of the donor's blood to see if you have any antibodies against your donor. **The goal is to have zero antibodies**.

When these factors characterize a *"healthy-enough-to-donate"* candidate to be an "incompatible" donor, an innovative program known as **Kidney Paired Donation (KPD)** can be considered.

In the KPD model, a sophisticated computer algorithm is used (by your transplant center working independently, or with national, or regional KPD programs) to find better matches. The objective is to "mix and match" incompatible donors and recipients *with* other incompatible recipients and donors, to find more compatible matches for all.

KPD was first utilized in 2000 by the New England Program for Kidney Exchange and became more widely accepted in 2007, after organ donation law caught up with trends in practice. KPD outcomes compelled transplant centers to optimize pair compatibility. This is called *"Compatible Shares."*

While there can be as few as two donors and two recipients in an exchange, the largest chain to date of this book printing involved a total of 70 individuals (35 recipients, 35 donors) and 26 transplant centers.

The diagram below illustrates two incompatible pairs:

Mother
Donor #1

Brother
Donor #2

Daughter
Rec #1

Sister
Rec #2

Source: *http://www.uwhealth.org/transplant*

Check with transplant centers in your area to learn more about KPD programs. If your center doesn't participate in KDP or doesn't offer a large national or regional pool, you might consider registering at another center.

You may also wish to register at multiple centers. For information on multiple center listings (see page 60); or visit: https://www.unos.org/wpcontent/uploads/unos/Multiple_Listing.pdf

Visit the Scientific Registry of Transplant Recipients (SRTR) *website* www.SRTR.org *for an active list of transplant centers and their waiting times. (Note: Centers located within the same region typically offer the same wait times.)*

Starting the Conversation

Since most healthy people don't realize they could possibly donate one of their kidneys (as a *living* donor)—and still live a normal, healthy life after donation; it's important to reference living donation opportunities when sharing your story. Here's a response to someone asking, "How have you been?" *or* "What's new?"

> *"Thanks for asking! I'm feeling extremely blessed these days. I was approved for a kidney transplant. I'll be able schedule the surgery as soon as I find someone willing to get tested (and approved) to be my living kidney donor."*

This quick information exchange has the potential of either abruptly ending the conversation—or creating interest and curiosity. When you sense interest or curiosity, continue to enlighten listeners by providing more information:

> *"Currently, my name resides on a transplant list with 100,000 people who are also waiting for a kidney from a deceased organ donor. In living kidney donation, there is no wait. Once the donor has been approved, the surgery can be scheduled."*

A thoughtful response to this conversation might be someone offering their best wishes. An even *more* thoughtful response might include an empathetic outreach while you're going through this difficult time. The best response, however, would be the listener asking: *"What qualifies someone to be a potential donor?"* or *"What type of testing is involved?"* This type of curiosity invites additional content sharing.

Regardless of how the conversation plays out, it's important to recognize that not all offers are the same. To that end, it's important to **recognize the difference between a desire to assist communication outreach *and* a true desire to donate.**

Don't rely on your interpretation of *what you think you heard* someone say. Always verify and clarify. Thank listeners for their compassion—and politely ask them to clarify what they meant by what they just said. This will minimize misunderstandings.

Likewise, never assume that a person is offering to give you one of their kidneys until they specifically say, "Maybe I could be your donor?" or "Perhaps I could give you one of my kidneys?"

When listeners imply they want to help you, ask for clarity on how they see themselves doing that. Provide examples as to how they can specifically assist you. Being an active listener also ensures communication accuracy. For example, you might repeat back what you thought you heard someone say in the form of a question: *"Do you mean you'd be willing to help me share my story?"* When you sense more interest, you might ask, *"Do you mean you'd be willing to get tested to see if you could donate a kidney to me?"*

This exchange clarifies the listener's intentions and minimizes misunderstandings and awkward assumptions.

Getting Down to Business – Scripting Your Story

While it may seem silly to script your story before you speak it, a written script can work wonders for taming storyteller nerves. Scripting also increases storytelling delivery and listener receptiveness, for a "deliverable win" for all.

The following steps will help you build your story:

Step 1: Pretend You Are a Screenwriter

Script your story as if you were writing a movie about your life, starting from the time you were diagnosed with chronic kidney disease. List the events in the order they occurred and highlight key turning points throughout that timeline.

Now, make the story bigger than yourself. Mention how many people are waiting for a kidney transplant and how most of them have been waiting for years on dialysis, hoping to get that call. Describe the physical and emotional hardships of dialysis. Be sure to mention that your goal is to avoid dialysis.

Don't worry about perfecting your script. You'll have time to do that later. For now, you just want to create a working draft.

After you've transcribed your story, you can underscore relevant elements to get your point across. These are your key *talking points*.

Now, read your script aloud to be sure your *talking points* add value to the story.

Repeat the process of reading your script until you feel you have something to work with. You can also run your script by a friend or family member to see how they perceive your telling of your story.

Observe your feelings while reading your story out loud. This process will help you communicate what you are trying to say more authentically. Don't worry if you feel embarrassed or awkward at first. It takes time to *"get your groove on."*

Step 2: Rehearse!

Rehearsing your story can give you more courage to share it. Rehearsing also protects you from unexpected triggers, like nervousness and other emotions that can disrupt your focus.

While rehearsing can make you a better communicator, it can also work against you if you attempt to *memorize* exact words. Your goal is to get familiar with your content, so you can communicate naturally, with good flow.

Try to imagine sharing your story in various situations. For example, you can create a list of the people you know, groups you belong to and events you plan to attend, that could offer you an opportunity to share your story.

Now, visualize your listeners responding to your story in those situations. Create a list of what you think "listener reactions" might be. Role-play these reactions in your mind. This exercise will help prepare you for a variety of responses.

Just as actors need to rehearse their lines to become intimately familiar with them, you need to do the same. Practice until the impromptu telling's of your story seem almost effortless.

Tell your story in a way that won't turn off listeners.

Keep in mind that your listeners will process your story in various ways. You might also want to keep in mind that an initial response to the telling of your story may be more about what's going on in the listener's life, than yours. Do not be disheartened if the closest people you know respond strangely or appear uninterested. *

Most people aren't aware of living kidney donation. Some feel dialysis is just as good, if not better than transplant. There's also a misconception about organ donation within certain religious groups. While views can vary, most major religions of the world do permit, allow and support organ donation.[9] Try to view things from a broader perspective.

Here are five examples of different listener types:

1. **Empathetic Ellie** offers a heartfelt ear. Ellie's life is crazy-busy. Would you consider her help unrealistic?

2. **Opinionated Oscar** recites hearsay about organ donation wrong-doing. Surprisingly, though, he's open to facts and alternative views. Do you continue to engage?

3. **Awkward Alice** isn't sure what to say, so she says nothing at all. Do you change the subject or share more?

4. **Interested Isaac** seems interested, but never circles back to you to see how he can help. Do you follow up?

5. **Bighearted Bob** sincerely wants to help you and asks for more information. Are you prepared to share next steps?

While it is not uncommon to distance yourself from insensitive responses, recognize your role is as much an educator as it is a story teller. Information empowers hope. Do not give up. Awkward reactions often lead you to other opportunities to engage in more promising conversations.

The key is to stay open-hearted in all conversations. Living kidney donation is not for everyone. When conversations become stagnant, embrace this awareness and move on.

Living kidney donation isn't for everyone.

Simply share your story from your heart with the goal of connecting to the hearts of your listeners. Use your script as a guide. This will keep emotions at bay and keep you on point.

Make your script bigger than yourself whenever you can. Include universal facts about organ donation and stay up-to-date on the information you're sharing.

For example, you can check the latest accounting of the number of people waiting on the kidney transplant list on *the United Network of Organ Sharing (UNOS's) OPTN* site: *http://optn.transplant.hrsa.gov/data/*

You can also search online for articles about preemptive transplantation and living kidney donation.

Step 3: Refine Message & Delivery

Practicing your story will help you refine the way you deliver the key points. Consider practicing in front of the mirror for immediate feedback.

While practicing, observe your body language and listen to the pitch of your voice. Do you sound relaxed or nervous? Does your story flow naturally or does it sound too rehearsed?

Adjust accordingly. After you have practiced several times in the mirror, step it up a notch and start practicing in front of people.

Start with new acquaintances so you won't worry about being judged. Test it out on store clerks, restaurant servers, telephone solicitors or waiting in line at the market or bank.

Other opportunities might include medical and dental assistants, your hygienist, manicurist, hair stylist or barber, postal workers, UPS and FedEx drivers, neighbors, bank tellers, your family's accountant and advisors.

When you're ready to advance to the next level of story sharing, practice with people closest to you. This would include a spouse or partner, parents and children, close friends and neighbors, co-workers, supervisors—and even your boss.

You might even invite select listeners to "role-play" with you and give you feedback.

Rehearsal sessions like these can help you become a better "teller" of your story, while also giving your listener-partners an opportunity to learn more about your situation.

As more people become aware of your need for a kidney, more opportunities will present themselves. This is how ordinary people consider extraordinary opportunities—like donating a kidney (as a living donor) to help someone in immediate need.

The telling of your story can be like a nuclear chain reaction. Each person who hears your story has an opportunity to give your story wings, by forwarding your story throughout their own social networks. They also get an opportunity to learn more and consider more—including testing to see if they might even be able to be your donor.

Step 4: Commit Once a Day

Commit to sharing your story to someone new at least once a day. This includes staying in touch with individuals who you've already shared your story with but haven't spoken to in a while. Create a victory log and feel good about your efforts.

You'll find tremendous potential in sharing your story. You'll also feel empowered by the courage it took for you to share it.

There are a lot of good-hearted people who are on the "lookout" for meaningful causes that make a difference. Many are still searching for what that might be. Your story could tap into their heartstring calling.

Just be mindful that while good-hearted people enjoy helping others, very few are looking to give someone one of their kidneys. That takes more discovery to build a connecting to this type of opportunity.

Step 5: Squelch Negative Thoughts

It's easy to get carried away with negative thoughts – in fact it's quite common. Do any of these statements sound familiar?

"I'll never find someone willing to donate a kidney to me."
"I can't put someone at risk for my own benefit."
"I'll be fine on dialysis. I don't need a transplant."

As you'll soon discover, receiving a kidney from someone else isn't just about you. It's a gift that gives donors tremendous joy in the giving. Even if you feel you aren't deserving—you can bet the "magnitude of gratitude" inside this remarkable exchange *is* bound to make you a *better* person.

The key is to make this assignment bigger than yourself. Every time you share your story you help 100,000 people who are on the same transplant list you're waiting on. For that reason, push yourself, even when you think you've shared your story enough times. Do it for "the crew" who are just like you.

Step 6: Use Sound Bites to Increase Awareness

Since living kidney donation is still a new concept for most, be open to engaging in thoughtful conversations about both living and deceased donation. This can help you explain how both options can be considered at different times throughout life.

Here are some thoughtful soundbites to consider:

- How living kidney donation allows a person to donate an organ and save a life today, while still considering deceased organ donation at the end of life.

- Expand communication by sharing links to informative content and videos. Here are a few links to get started:

  - https://youtu.be/egKpspvgJDY

  - https://www.livingbank.org/organ-donation/living-donation

  - http://asts.org/resources/living-kidney-donation-english#.WDy0PeYrKUk

  - http://www.cpmc.org/advanced/kidney/LivingDonation/

  - http://www.hopkinsmedicine.org/transplant/living_donors

  - http://www.barnabashealth.org/Specialty-Services/Kidney-Care/The-Living-Donor-Institute.aspx

- http://www.bidmc.org/Centers-and-Departments/Departments/Transplant-Institute/Kidney/Information-for-Living-Kidney-Donors.aspx

- Dispel deceased organ donation myths that have led people to believe that all attempts to save their life will not be made if they are an organ donor.

- Reference the national organ shortage and include the fact that not all consented donors can donate at the time of death, due to family overriding the donor's wishes, or from medical disqualification.

- **Encourage open discussions on all donation systems**. In the U.S. we have what is called *Assumed Declination*.

  In other words, if there is no evidence of *expressed consent* from the deceased donor, it is <u>assumed</u> that the patient is **not** an organ donor. *When this is the case, viable organs cannot be used to save lives.*

  In other countries like Spain, Austria, and Belgium, an Opt-Out plan is followed under a *Presumed Consent* law. This means if there is no evidence of *expressed declination* or "opting out" from organ donation from the deceased, they are presumed to be an organ donor, providing their organs and tissue qualify.

  The difference here is that individuals must document their *opposition to organ donation*, rather than their *willingness to donate*. <u>Since there is no action required to be a donor under this system, organs are often more readily available.</u>

  All too often, well-intentioned people never get around to talking about their intentions or recording their intentions.

Whether it be reluctance, procrastination *or* just not making it a high enough priority, a "could-be" organ-donor misses the opportunity of potentially saving up to eight lives—or helping a total of 50 lives through organ *and* tissue donation.

- Another topic to consider might include discussions on supporting ***zero financial impact*** for living kidney donors. This might cover discussions on managing a donor's out-of-pocket costs, like travel expenses, home care assistance during recovery, and lost wages for time off work.

Currently, under the National Organ Transplant Act, 42, U.S.C. 274e (2002) (NOTA), enacted in 1984:

> ***"It is a federal crime to knowingly acquire, receive or otherwise transfer any human organ for valuable consideration for use in human transplantation if the transfer affects interstate commerce."***
> (i.e. meaning goods or money)

The maximum fine for this violation is $50,000 or a five-year imprisonment term, or both. Fortunately, there are exclusions to valuable consideration restrictions. [10]

The expenses listed below are **excluded** from the National Organ Transplant Act punishable crimes statement:

> ### EXCLUSIONS:
> **"Reasonable Payments Associated with Expenses for Travel, Housing and Lost Wages."**

On the bright side, new legislative initiatives continue to be introduced to remove these financial disincentives for living kidney donors. They include:

- **Living Donor Protection Act of 2017** proposes to prohibit discrimination based on an individual's status as a living organ donor in the offering, issuance, cancellation, coverage, price, or any other condition of a life insurance policy, disability insurance policy, or long-term care insurance policy.
https://www.congress.gov/bill/115th-congress/house-bill/1270

- **FMLA UPDATE:** The Department of Labor clarified language on August 28, 2018, that the surgery for living organ donation qualifies for leave under the Family Medical Leave Act (FMLA).
https://www.dol.gov/whd/opinion/FMLA/2018/2018_08_28_2A_FMLA.pdf

- **Organ Donor Clarification Act of 2016** was introduced to clarify that certain reimbursements are not considered "valuable consideration," but rather reimbursements for expenses a donor incurs.
https://www.congress.gov/bill/114th-congress/house-bill/5344/text

Note: The National Kidney Foundation is a strong supporter of policies that protect living donors from financial hardships and extend benefits of the Family Medical Leave Act to ensure job security during surgical and recovery periods. [11]

It should also be noted that a kidney transplant pays for itself in less than two years; saving an average of $745,000/per patient in medical costs over ten years, by eliminating dialysis dependence.

How to Become a Donor-Magnet® Pro

Step 1: Communicate from Heart

Striking up a conversation about your need for a kidney can be emotionally daunting. When you add the fear of speaking, to the fear of listener rejection, the thought of sharing your story can be paralyzing.

If, however, you share your story from your heart, your heart will override those little voices in your head that want you to believe you're incapable of attaining this goal.

To communicate from your heart, means to communicate with empathy and positive intent. It also implies a connection to self. You can get a palpable sense of "coming from heart" by simply placing your hand over your heart while speaking. Test it out now.

Coming from heart invites a deeper, more honest conversation and bond. It can transform people, situations and relationships to feel more connected by their emotions.

Coming from heart is not just about what you say, it's how you say it. It's not the words alone. It's your tone, facial expressions and body language attached to the words. It's also about observing your listeners' response. What is their body language communicating?

Look for clues. Is it appropriate to continue the dialogue or shift gears? When the stakes are as high as they are in this type of conversation, listener receptiveness is key.

Coming from heart is also about being prepared, respectful and not needy. *Share your situation in a factual way, without undue pressure. Your job is to increase awareness. You don't want to encourage overly eager individuals to jump too fast to volunteer.*

Assume most volunteers do not understand the full scope of what's involved. Whether someone thinks they want to be your donor or they simply want to help you share your story, it's important to encourage independent discovery. While you'll need to provide a general overview; avoid a conflict of interest by simply referring interested donors to your transplant center.

Interested donors may also benefit from speaking with other living kidney donors (see: Mentoring & Coaching, next page). *They can also visit living donor information websites:* https://transplantfirst.org/go/living-heroes/; *https://www.kidney.org/transplantation/livingdonors/biggive*

Step 2: Enlist & Mobilize Donor Outreach Advocates

Let's face it. It's hard to share your story *all* by yourself. Since there's more power in numbers, consider enlisting an army of spokespersons to serve on your *Donor Outreach Team.*

You can do this by inviting friends and other family members to become part of your *network,* so they can help you increase awareness and expand your search for potential donors.

Some of your best cheerleaders will be those who wished they could have been your donor but for various medical or personal reasons were unable to proceed. Their genuine desire to want to help you creates a stronger connection to your cause and a more compelling story-share in outreach.

Be sure your team of *Donor Outreach Advocates* are intimately familiar with your story. They also need to know general information about living kidney donation and your transplant center. It's best to set boundaries on how much information they can share directly *and* when it's best to refer to your transplant center for more specific answers to questions.

Your *Donor Outreach Team* is most effective when they can:

(1) Create interest and curiosity
(2) Answer basic questions and refer detailed questions out
(3) Follow up to ensure all interested parties connected with your transplant center and questions have been answered

Step 3: Seek Mentors & Coaches

Working with a patient mentor, advocate or coach, who truly understands the physical and emotional side of what it's like to be a patient in need of a kidney transplant, can be quite helpful.

It's important to connect with individuals who have walked this path before you and are willing to share their experience. There are reputable organizations that offer kidney patient and living donor mentoring at no cost. They include:

- The National Kidney Foundation's Peers Program
  https://www.kidney.org/patients/peers

- The American Transplant Foundation's Mentorship Program http://www.americantransplantfoundation.org

- The PKD Foundation's Mentor Program (*Launching soon*)

You can also ask individuals who have had successful transplant journeys if they would be willing to share their experiences with you. Attempt to match yourself with individuals who have achieved what you hope to achieve.

Peer mentors are often restricted from giving advice. Their role is to share their experience to help you reflect on your own journey. If you are seeking specific (non-medical) advice or strategies, it would be best to contact a kidney patient *coach*.

Coaches share more than their personal experiences, by offering feedback and suggesting action steps to keep you motivated. They can also be your role-play partner, providing perspective and ideas on your written and spoken messages. Additionally, they can direct you to helpful resources and books to boost your awareness campaign.

Unlike volunteer mentors, coaches offer services for a fee. Visit: http://www.theproactivepath.com/kidneypatientcoach/

Step 4: Create Your Outreach Campaign

Having a strategic plan to expand the scope of your team's message will be key to campaign success. That said, it is best to start your campaign with organizational structure.

Consider these guidelines to facilitate this assignment:

- **Use spreadsheets to stay organized.** Use individual spreadsheets to keep track of activities performed by you and everyone serving on your *Donor Outreach Team*.

- **Don't limit the list.** The list should include all the people you know who might help you network your story. Expand your list beyond family members, close friends and healthy individuals. You never know who someone might know.

- **Include co-workers, associations & memberships.** Include co-workers, colleagues and even your boss. Also consider individuals you know through professional organizations, social and community groups, club buddies and people who share your same hobbies or engage in your favorite sports activities. Include places of worship, alumni, sorority and fraternity connections. Expand your network by seeking to volunteer with other people who like to volunteer. Don't forget to seek opportunities to volunteer for police officers, firefighters—and the selfless heroes who keep our country safe.

- **Don't assume.** Don't prejudge individuals on how compassionate or busy their lives are. As many kidney transplant recipients can attest, the most promising offers often came from those they least expected.

- **Track it.** Ensure follow up and prevent redundancy by tracking your work. This includes keeping a contact list of individual outreach names, so you and your team can track the emails and letters that have been sent to these individuals. It also identifies what type of letter was sent and the date of each communication, along with subsequent follow up. *See page 66 for full page layout.*

CONTACT LIST NAMES	EMAIL ADDRESS	SENT BY	LETTER TYPE (DOC CODE)	DATE SENT	FOLLOW UP

Step 5: Communicate in Third-Person

Now that you've created your list, it's time to transform your story into a third-person communication piece. Third-person communications are written about you (and in this case, by you), but expressed as if they were written by someone else. Incorporate your heart and soul into your third-person communications message to ensure your heart can still be felt.

Write your message as an information piece, not a solicitation piece. You don't want readers to feel pressured by a plea for help. Remember to include an introduction and closing line that includes a way to contact the 'third person.'

Be mindful of how you'd respond if you were on the other side of this communication exchange. Write your message the way you'd prefer to read about *someone else's* need.

Enlist the help of your *Donor Outreach Advocates* when writing the letter. Ask them to proof your letter and share suggestions for improvement. As you work together to finalize the letter, ask those serving on your *Donor Outreach Advocate Team* if they would be willing to customize the letter and send it out to their family, friends and colleagues, as a *third-party* voice speaking on your behalf.

The beauty behind third-party communications, is that they avoid a direct plea for help, which can be awkward and off-putting. It is far more effective to have someone speak on your behalf, than to ask for something directly.

Your communications should be easy to read and understand. They need to also include facts and a compassionate call to action. **(See sample template letters, starting on page 48.)**

As previously stated, it is always best if your communications aren't just about YOU. Paint a broader picture by speaking on behalf of *all* those in need. Include facts such as: (1) though there are risks to any surgery, living kidney donors can live a full, vibrant life with just one kidney, (2) all medical expenses are covered by the recipient's medical insurance, and (3) living kidney donors earn accelerated waitlist status, should they ever need a kidney transplant in the future.

Whether you write the outreach communication as if one of your *Donor Outreach Team members* was writing it for you; or they write it themselves, be sure to put your eyes on the document several times before it goes out. This will maximize message accuracy and engagement.

Step 6: Before Sending or Posting Content

Ensure your outreach team is using the same talking points that you are using before sending emails and posting content. They should also be mindful of proper online etiquette.

For email, this includes a policy of not disclosing the names and addresses of the parties to whom you are group emailing. You can keep your "send to" names and email addresses confidential by creating an undisclosed list, or blind copying the group in the "BCC" area. This is recommended to respect list privacy. The goal is to minimize email address exposure.

In both email and social posts, attempt to use *"catchy"* introductions to grab your reader's attention. You can also boost message attraction by adding colorful art, video messages and links. Proofing your letter several times before sending is also important, as it helps you minimize typos, improve sentence structure and phrasing. The more "eyes" you can put on your communications, the clearer the message.

Step 7: Using Social Media, Websites & Blogs

As many of us have experienced over the years, the internet offers a wonderful communication space for dialoguing. Platforms such as Facebook, Twitter, LinkedIn, YouTube, Instagram, Tumblr, Google+ and Snapchat provide wonderful opportunities to expand story-reach. There's even a study that created a smartphone App for finding living donors: http://www.nephjc.com/news/2016/9/17/app4donor

One word of caution relative to social media. Some transplant centers have shared concerns about accepting donors who met their intended recipient through social media. That said, it would be wise to check with your transplant center to avoid disappointments or lost time.

Social media can hold a high degree of disappointment. For example, it is not uncommon for someone to indicate interest and then disappear. Yet, disappointments of this kind can also happen with individuals you've known for years. It's best to encourage individuals to get tested as a "potential back-up" when someone is being tested at the time of their offer.

You might also want to consider having your own website or blog. Template-ready **websites** or **blogs** can be done much easier now that there are cost effective DIY programs offering affordable hosting fees. Be sure to include your contact information and links to your transplant center as well.

Health journal websites, like www.CaringBridge.org, can also be considered as a means for keeping everyone informed.

Step 8: Increasing Media Exposure

Tap into broadcasting resources by connecting with local media. Local media can include newspapers, radio and TV stations. The media loves human-interest stories, so search for medical updates that can humanize their news pieces and add relevant value to their reporting assignments.

Step 9: Signs, Message Boards & Cards

Using *donate life* **license plates, car magnet messaging and highway billboards** can be quite effective for community advertising purposes. Here's two examples:

EXTERIOR CAR SIGNS & MAGNETS

HIGHWAY BILLBOARDS

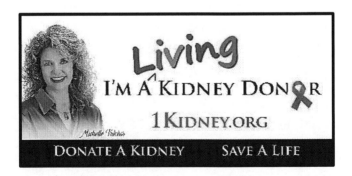

MESSAGE BOARDS: Consider places of worship and other groups that offer digital and physical message boards. **Here's how one example might read:**

Would You Like to Play a Part in One of Life's Greatest "Pay It Forward" Opportunities by Becoming a Living Kidney Donor?
A person from our community is in urgent need of a kidney transplant. Her/his hope is to spend more time with her/his grandchildren. If you are in good health, between the ages of 18 and 65, we'd love to tell you more about this process.
Please call the Patient's Advocate: 555-345-6789
or email: *grace@exampleonly.com*

CONTACT-STORY CARDS (CSC's) are like business cards, but instead of listing business information, they offer personal contact information for you and your transplant center—and details about your situation. CSC's provide a quick exchange of detailed information which invites continued engagement.

The example below illustrates relevant contact information (with your photo) on the front, and a snapshot about your need for a transplant and hope for finding a donor on the back.

FRONT   BACK

Step 10: Organizing Social Events & Fundraising

One example of what you could consider, would be to *host* an event, or *volunteer* at an existing event that could potentially help you increase need awareness.

Social Awareness Events. Hosting a social event to increase awareness can be quite effective. For these types of venues, you could invite friends to join you for an informative wine and cheese gathering in your home. You can also encourage your friends to bring a friend or two along. After everyone has settled in, call the group's attention so you can formally explain your event's cause.

Kickstart the conversation by sharing the facts behind the nation's organ shortage, the wait for a kidney from a deceased donor, along with your need for a transplant and your hope for a living kidney donor. Ask your guests to make suggestions on how you could create buzz about your story. Make it fun. Have prizes for the best ideas and give everyone a door prize with your story contact card attached.

Fundraising and Causes. If a foundation or support group for your specific kidney disease exists, you can fundraise to support their mission, or create your own group *or* cause. Check out Facebook groups to start *or* join a cause. Another option would be to start a Go Fund Me campaign (https://www.gofundme.com). If you choose to do this, be sure everyone's aware of transaction fees and charges.

Offer to emcee someone else's event or ask the emcee to mention your story during their opening and closing remarks to humanize the event. You can seek these types of opportunities through health outreach organizations.

Family, high school or association reunions are perfect venues for sharing your story with people who have history with you. Think about it. No one has seen you in years, possibly decades, and everyone will be asking *"What have you been up to these days?"*

Schedule a coffee or lunch date with a fellow employee, your boss or old acquaintances who might be willing to help you share your story.

Note: If you fear that your job might be in jeopardy after disclosing your kidney disease diagnosis, assure listeners that your condition is not affecting your work at this time (but, only if that statement is true). You can assure them that you'll be the first to inform them, in the event that your circumstances change.

If a person responds unfavorably to your story, simply apologize for being so talkative. Strange reactions can often be triggered for various reasons, much of which have nothing to do with you or your need. Keep in mind that all **responses are not a reflection of the relationship people have with you, but rather the relationship they have with themselves.**

If listeners say nothing, this is not a bad sign. Living kidney donation is not for everyone—and everyone will process what they heard in different ways. Give them time to process.

When it becomes clear that someone is not comfortable listening to you talk about your situation, consider their response as a blessing in disguise. They're basically giving you a heads-up that they're not someone you can count on, so don't try. While their disinterest may seem unkind, recognize this "sneak preview" as a way to prevent future disappointments. Set these individuals free (n your mind) and allow yourself to move on.

Just keep telling your story as often as you can and to as many people as possible. But only expand on your story elements when you sense the listener is interested in learning more. Relentlessly follow these steps and you'll soon take on the *superpowers* of a "Donor Magnet® Pro.

Step 11: The Power of Your Intention

The power of your intention is fueled by what you believe your life would look like after you achieve your end-game goal. When you visualize the result of that end-game goal, you'll begin to sense the power behind your *intention*.

Intentions follow the belief that "likes attract likes." If you think positive thoughts about your future, you're more likely to attract a more positive outcome. Likewise, if you think negative thoughts, you're more likely to attract a less desirable outcome. This magnetic model is known as *the law of attraction.*

The law of attraction comes from a new thought movement dating back to the early 1900s. Highly respected author, Napoleon Hill, directly references the law of attraction in his 1928 book, *The Law of Success in 16 Lessons*. You may be familiar with one of Hill's bestsellers, *Think and Grow Rich*. In this book, Hill explains the importance of controlling one's thoughts to achieve greater success. He describes the power of our thoughts and their ability to attract other thoughts.

For this reason, we must all be mindful of our thoughts and the words we use to communicate them. While we may not be able to stop all negative thinking, we can nip those thoughts in the bud by consciously paying more attention.

To that end, as soon as you catch yourself in the act of negative mind chatter, hit the "pause button." While pausing, *flip* your negative thought or statement into a more positive expression or desire (even if you don't fully believe what you're saying at the time).

Don't worry about having to completely "buy into" this process initially. After you've had a chance to witness the good that can come from these new behaviors, it will naturally become more believable.

You Can Live Your Life by What You Don't Have *or*
You Can Live Your Life by What You Hope to Attract *into* It.

When you flip negative mind chatter into positive statements of belief, you're re-training your mind to turn negative thoughts into more positive forms of belief.

Start by *flipping* negative statements like "No one is ever going to offer to be my donor!" or, "I'll never find a living kidney donor healthy enough to get approved" by replacing those statements with examples like these:

"I'm so grateful to have a donor in testing—and a handful of back up donors standing by."

"My living kidney donor was approved to donate a kidney to me—and all is a go!"

How to Write an Intention Statement

Written statements of intention are the most powerful way to attract results. In other words, you can't just think or say the words verbally. You need to write your intentions down on paper and read them often.

Here's a few ideas to get you started:

- List three things you'd like to attract into your life.
- Change your hopes and desires *into* existing blessings: *"I hope to receive ..."* would become *"I now have...."*

Your intention statement can also include other dreams outside your living kidney donor transplant goal. For example, you might want to be more open, more curious, more giving, or engaged in the present moment. It can also include your general health and happiness and family's health and happiness, travels and adventures.

While your intention statement doesn't have to be exclusive to your transplant goals, your transplant success needs to be the core focus of this exercise.

Do not worry if your intention statement might sound somewhat foolish or overly confident.

That's the point of this exercise. You need to advance your level of believability.

The only person judging you is YOU. You are the sole creator, reader, story teller—and benefactor of the outcomes you attract. Read your written intention statement often to increase momentum behind your beliefs.

The key is to believe that your intentions are not only possible, but that they already exist. The mere exercise of defining your intentions on paper (in the present tense) is what will create a "magnetic field of thoughts" that can attract good your way.

The following tips will help you create a powerful written intention statement.

Intention Checklist

☐ Get inside the time machine of tomorrow to see your ideal scenario happening right before your eyes. Once you're there, describe your ideal donor offer.

☐ Summon a feeling of immense gratitude while watching this movie play out in your mind. Create a tender scene where your ideal donor unfolds their offer. Accept this viewing as if it were a true accounting of your real-life experience.

☐ Visualize a positive interaction with your transplant center. Imagine they just called to tell you that your donor has been approved to donate one of their kidneys to you.

☐ Hear their voice confirming this is true. Repeat their words aloud: *"Your donor has been approved!"*

☐ Now try to articulate what you envisioned into the written word. Write it out as fact, rather than a wish or dream. While this process is challenging, it's well worth the effort.

*Do not worry about getting the words perfect on the first or even third "go around." This is a working document that can be refined multiple times.

- [ ] Print out your first draft. Read the draft and smooth out the rough spots. Repeat this refining process until you feel you have it close enough to make it official.

- [ ] Post your intention statement in several places so it is visible upon waking, brushing your teeth and talking on the phone.

- [ ] Print a miniature version for your wallet and carry it with you everywhere.

Even if you feel this process is *silly* – give it a go anyway. You have nothing to lose but possible regret.

Believe Your Best Scenario is Not Only Possible; Believe It's Happening Now!
This is the Path to Limitless Potential.

Success Tips in Review

1. **Script your story.** Practice the telling of your story and share it with as many people as you can *and* as often as you can.

2. **Expand your outreach** efforts through email, message boards, story contact cards, flyers, social media posts and social events, including fundraising for awareness causes.

3. **Enlist advocates to help share your story**. Invite family, friends and co-workers to serve on your *Donor Outreach Team* to help you expand story reach.

   Remember, you don't have to go it alone.

4. **Consider working with a mentor or private coach.**
   A mentor can provide experience and insight. A coach can provide strategic advice and help you stay focused, motivated and on task.

5. **Create a written intention statement to declare your beliefs and read it daily.** Believe that you already have everything you need. Live by this belief and witness positive reactions coming your way. *(You can use the worksheets in the back of this book to record quick thoughts and ideas.)*

6. **Stay in-touch with potential donors.** Don't assume potential donors understand the scope of what they have offered to do for you. Engage in thoughtful conversations as often as you feel appropriate and encourage them to do the same. Here are some examples:

   a) Encourage potential donors to get all their questions addressed by transplant center personnel.
   b) Encourage evaluation tests be scheduled efficiently to minimize travel time and delays in communication.
   c) Encourage your transplant center to give potential donors an idea of when they can expect to hear back.
   d) Encourage potential donors to stay in touch with <u>you</u> to minimize the heartache of "second guessing."

Keeping Yourself Healthy While You Wait

You can maximize your wait time and keep yourself healthy by remaining mindful of these tips:

- Follow the diet your healthcare team recommends
- Do not drink alcohol or smoke
- Avoid sick people and large crowds
- Keep your weight within the range recommended
- Follow your recommended exercise routines
- Take medicines as prescribed
- Report all medications & supplement changes
- Report new *(or worsening)* medical problems
- Follow up with your regular doctors and transplant team
- Keep your contact information current
- Be proactively engaged with your donor outreach team

Staying Positive and Proactive

If your motivation levels tend to fluctuate *or* you tend to procrastinate, simply catch yourself and push your mental "reset" button. The simple fact that you caught yourself derailed, can shift you back on track. Start by doing something positive. Go for a walk *or* do something nice for someone else. As a daily ritual, read these statements to keep your intentions focused:

1. I intend to share my story often.
2. I intend to build and assist my *Donor Outreach Team*.
3. I intend to keep myself healthy and proactively engaged.
4. I intend to be grateful, even during disappointing times.
5. I intend to think positive and believe *all* things are possible.

"We Must All Suffer One of Two Things: The Pain of Discipline *or* The Pain of Regret."

-Jim Rohn, Motivational Speaker

EmPOWER UP!

As we approach the end of this patient guidebook,
I leave you with some mindful thoughts:

Recognize, that while you can't go back and start a new beginning, you have the power to create a better ending.

See this journey as an opportunity to become a top contender in one of the most important fights of your life.

Be willing to open your heart and allow others to give their "Best Self" to <u>YOU</u>, so you can give your "Best Self" to others!

Now is <u>not</u> a time to stop doing.
Now is the time to ignite your Donor Magnet® Superpowers—and attract your ideal living kidney donor.

You've got this!

A Friend's Post

I am posting this message to share a serious medical challenge that our friend [friend's name] is facing right now, to see if you can help.

[Insert name] is in urgent need of a kidney transplant and the current wait for a replacement kidney from a deceased organ donor is about 5 years.

Typically, when someone is dealing with a critical health problem, all we can do is support them—and believe me, that's needed here too. Yet this time there is an opportunity to save, improve and extend a life.

With 100,000 people waiting on a list for a kidney from a deceased donor, and over a dozen people dying every day while waiting, I'm worried sick about (friend's name) future.

I'm now on a mission to help end this life-threatening wait for [friend's name]. My goal is to find [friend's name] a healthy living kidney donor, so she/he can get this much-needed transplant and secure a better, and longer life.

Since I'm unable to donate one of my kidneys, I'm doing all that I can to find others who could.

Living donors can end the wait.

There have been more than 149,000 living kidney donor surgeries performed, so this is not a new concept. My hope is that you might know individuals who might be interested in learning more about this life-saving opportunity.

If you would like more information about the donor screening process, the surgery, and recovery, please contact [insert friend's name] transplant center (see contact information below).

You may also contact me as well, as I'd invite the opportunity to tell you more. I'd also like to hear your thoughts on what you think might be helpful.

Thank you for taking the time to read this post. Fire away with questions (if you have any) and please forward this post onto others so we can increase awareness for all those in need.

[Your Signature Here]

(Your contact information below)

_____

_____

_____

(Your Friend's Transplant Center's Contact Information & Links)

_____

_____

_____

Family & Friends – Preemptive Transplant

Dear Family and Friends,

While most of you know I have kidney disease, you may not be aware that my kidney function has started to rapidly decline. It was not until my doctor reviewed my recent lab work that discussions advanced to my only two survival options—dialysis or transplant.

During those discussions, my doctor encouraged me to find a living kidney donor, so I could avoid the need for dialysis before getting a transplant (which is the best option, known as a preemptive transplant).

Since time is not on my side, I accepted this assignment to secure my future and live a better quality of life. I know my condition has also taken a toll on friends and family, so I'm pledging to do whatever it takes to offer you guys a better version of me too!

This new awareness helped me find the courage to share what I've been learning about the value of getting a transplant from a living kidney donor. I guess you could say that I'm on a mission to help all those in need by getting this information more well-known. If you choose to read on, you'll see how this "awareness wave" unfolds.

Why Not Dialysis?

Dialysis is a mechanical process that attempts to mimic kidney function by mechanically filtering the blood. This is a long drawn out process that lasts for several hours at a time, several days a week, if not daily.

This treatment option requires a surgical procedure to allow the dialysis unit to gain access to my blood stream or belly lining, depending on the type of dialysis performed. From what I've heard, it is not uncommon to require multiple surgeries to keep the "access line" functioning properly and free from infection.

Dialysis also requires a very strict diet and liquid limitations, including water. I've also heard that it can be painful, nauseating and cause days of lingering fatigue.

While this concerns me greatly, the most daunting thing about dialysis is that it only provides 10-13% of normal kidney function, which is considerably lower than what I have now.

Why A Kidney Transplant Offers More

A kidney transplant is considered the best option because it provides 24/7 function that offers a much longer and better life expectancy. A kidney transplant doesn't require a demanding schedule or diet and fluid restrictions.

It does, however, require a major surgery and a new kidney; followed by life-long immune-reducing medications to prevent organ rejection.

Why Not Wait for a *Deceased* Organ Donor's Kidney?

The wait for a deceased donor's kidney in [your state here] can be [insert number here] years. With nearly [insert number here] people waiting for a transplant—and roughly [insert number here] additional names added annually, I fear I'd be on dialysis for quite some time.

And while dialysis can extend life for those waiting, there are serious risks long term. Those risks include developing infections and other health conditions that can lead to less desirable outcomes and illnesses that often terminate transplant candidacy.

Why Consider a Kidney from a *Living* Kidney Donor?

I am told the best way to avoid dialysis (or end the need for dialysis for those already on dialysis) is to get a kidney from a living donor. Living kidney donors advance transplant timelines by removing the need to wait in line for a deceased donor's kidney.

Transplants performed with kidneys from living donors often function better, last longer and respond more favorably than deceased donor kidneys.

These new discoveries have been triggering me to learn more, do more and share what I've been learning with others.

Spreading the Word

Please accept this letter as an open invitation to join the "help (insert name) find a living kidney donor" team, by sharing my story in social media, like Facebook. (I can provide a sample for posts).

Even if you can't join this effort, know that you're helping me by just reading this letter. The way I look at it, the more people I can educate, the more awareness I can create—and the more awareness created, the greater the chance of finding potential living kidney donors.

For those who would like to learn a bit more about the living kidney donation process, please contact my transplant center (see information below) for more specific information on the screening process and the phases that follow, like testing, the surgical procedure, risk and recovery timelines.

If you made it down this far in the letter, know that there's no need to respond. The time you took to read this update is a gift in and of itself.

With immense hope and gratitude,

[Your signature here]

Email Address
Cell Phone Number
Website (If Applicable)
Transplant Center Name, City, State
Transplant Center Call-in Number
Transplant Center Online Links

Family & Friends - Dialysis Patient

Dear friends and family,

I'm writing this letter to share an encouraging update. While most of you know my kidneys are damaged and that I've been struggling for several (insert months/years) on dialysis, I've been told there's a good chance I could advance to transplant if I'm able to find a suitable living kidney donor.

One of the biggest challenges in waiting for a transplant is surviving the long wait for a kidney from a deceased donor. With approximately 100,000 people waiting for a deceased donor's kidney and an average wait of five years—I now see that I'm putting my life at risk by doing nothing more than waiting. Today I'm choosing to do more.

My doctors and nurses are encouraging me to find a living kidney donor who can end my wait for a transplant, so I can live a better quality of life. While I believe I deserve this, this is not just about me anymore. I know the toll dialysis has had on my friends and family, and I want to offer you all a better version of me too.

This new awareness helped me find the courage to share what I've been learning about the value of getting a transplant from a living kidney donor. I guess you could say that I'm on a mission to help all those in need by getting this information more well-known. If you choose to read on, you'll see how this "awareness wave" unfolds.

Life on Dialysis

As many of you may know, dialysis is a mechanical process that attempts to mimic kidney function by mechanically filtering the blood. This is a long drawn out process that lasts for several hours at a time, several days a week, if not daily. This treatment option requires a surgical procedure, so the machine's filtering process can gain access to my bloodstream or belly lining. From what I've been told, it's not uncommon to require multiple surgeries to keep the "access line" functioning properly and free from infection.

Dialysis also requires a very strict diet and liquid limitations, including water. I've also heard that treatments can be painful, nauseating and cause days of lingering fatigue. While this concerns me greatly, the most discouraging thing about dialysis is that it only provides about 13% of normal kidney function, which is less than what I have right now—and I already feel like I'm running on empty.

Working Towards a Kidney Transplant

While getting a transplant requires a major surgery and a "donated" kidney in order to perform the surgery—it also requires life-long immune-reducing medications, to ensure our body doesn't reject the new kidney. Nonetheless, transplants are the best option for those who medically qualify. When I start to imagine a replacement kidney that could provide me 24/7 function (*without real* diet or fluid restrictions, or spending endless hours on a dialysis machine), it seems like a fairytale. Yet, this type of life-enhancing fairytale is worth every ounce of effort in helping it come true.

A kidney transplant from a deceased organ donor.

Unfortunately, the average wait for a deceased donor's kidney can be 5 years. With nearly 100,000 people waiting for a transplant—and roughly 35,000 additional names annually, I fear I'd be risking my life waiting on dialysis for a kidney from a deceased donor.

I also understand that even though dialysis can add years to my life, most of that extra time would be spent on dialysis. I'm also told that there can be serious risks long-term, like developing infections and other health conditions that can lead to less desirable outcomes and illnesses. Moreover, some of those conditions could disqualify me from ever receiving a transplant.

A kidney transplant from a living kidney donor.

I am told the best way to advance to transplant and end my need for dialysis is by receiving a kidney from a *living* donor. Living donors are individuals who are healthy enough to donate one of their two kidneys (while they are still living)—while expecting to live a full and meaningful life after donation.

While receiving a kidney from a living donor can eliminate my wait for a transplant, there are additional benefits to be gained. For example, it has been well documented that transplants performed with kidneys from living donors often function better, last longer and respond more favorably, than kidneys from deceased donors. These new discoveries have triggered me to learn more, do more and share what I've learned with others.

Spreading the Word

Please accept this letter as an open invitation to join the "help (insert name) find a living kidney donor" team, by sharing my story in social media, like Facebook. (I can provide a sample for posts).

Even if you can't join this effort, know that you're helping me by just reading this letter. The way I look at it, the more people I can educate, the more awareness I can create—and the more awareness created, the greater the chance of finding potential living kidney donors.

For those who would like to learn a bit more about the living kidney donation process, please contact my transplant center (see information below) for more specific information on the screening process and the phases that follow, like testing, the surgical procedure, risk and recovery timelines.

If you made it down this far in the letter, know that there's no need to respond. The time you took to read this update is a gift in and of itself.

With immense hope and gratitude,

[Your signature here]

Email Address
Cell Phone Number
Website (If Applicable)
Transplant Center Name, City, State
Transplant Center Call-in Number
Transplant Center Online Links

Client Letters & Company Newsletters

Dear Clients and Associates,

Allow me to apologize in advance for using our professional contacts for this personal outreach. Unfortunately, we've exhausted our resources *and* a life is at stake.

You may recall working with [insert name] over the years. Unfortunately, [insert name] has been diagnosed with chronic kidney failure and is in urgent need of a kidney transplant. The wait for a kidney from a deceased donor can be several years. I'm hoping to spare [insert name] from a hard life on dialysis.

The only way to end [insert name] wait for a kidney on the national transplant list— (a list with over 100,000 people), is by getting a kidney from a living donor. My hope is that this message might inspire readers to share [insert name's] need for a transplant and help us with our search for a living kidney donor. Ultimately, our goal is to find individuals who would be willing to consider testing on [insert name's] behalf. If, by chance, you'd like to learn more about the donor testing process, please feel free to contact [insert name's] transplant center for additional information.

[Include Your Contact Information & Transplant Center Information Below]

COMPANY NEWSLETTERS:

Another method of business outreach can be accomplished through an organization's newsletter. Here's an example posting:

"Please join us in sending good thoughts and wishes to one of your fellow associates, (insert name). (Insert employee's name) is in urgent need of a kidney transplant and the only way to end her/his wait is by getting a kidney from a living kidney donor. If you'd like to learn more about what this process involves, please contact (insert employee's name's) transplant center (insert center name and website link). You may also contact (Insert employee's name) directly. *Note: You may be eligible to take time off work under FMLA. Contact our HR department to learn more.*

Social Media Posts

POST ABOUT A FRIEND:

I'm spreading the word about my friend [insert friend's name] who is in desperate need of a kidney transplant. Currently, there are more than 100,000 people waiting in line ahead of [insert friend's name] on the national transplant list, and the average wait for a kidney from a deceased donor is 5 years. [Insert person's name] needs a kidney today and can't wait that long without risking her/his life. Since I'm not an ideal candidate, I'm hoping to connect with others who might be interested in getting tested to see if they could qualify to donate one of their two kidneys to [insert friends name]. Want to learn more first? Visit [transplant center's name] website [insert link] or call them directly with your questions [insert phone line]. I'd also invite a conversation. You can contact me on my private email [insert contact information here].

POST ABOUT YOURSELF:

While most of you know I have kidney disease, you may not know that I'm now in urgent need of a kidney transplant. Unfortunately, 100,000 people are already waiting on the national transplant list— and the average wait for a kidney (from a deceased donor) is 5 years. While this is a bit awkward for me to talk about, my doctor's and nurses are encouraging me to reach out to friends and family to see if they can help me search for a living kidney donor match. If you'd like to learn more, visit my transplant center's website [insert link here] or call them directly with your questions [insert contact info here]. For those of you who are moved to re-post this message, I thank you from the bottom of my heart (and kidneys) for increasing my odds for a better tomorrow.

Potential Donor's Announcement

Dear Family & Friends,

I have something to say that might sound a bit shocking to you. So, before I share it, I want you to know that my decision was not based on misguided thinking. I've done my homework and I feel confident about my decision to help someone in need.

Over the years, I've wanted to contribute to the world in a more meaningful way but wasn't sure how I could do that. Well now I do. I've discovered an opportunity to become a living kidney donor and extend the quality of life and remaining years for someone in need.

I realize this announcement may take time to digest, especially the part that involves the risk of me being involved in a surgical procedure. Though the risk is small, it doesn't make it any less real. I would expect you to have concerns because you care.

And, even though I don't know if I'd qualify to be a living kidney donor yet, it might put your mind at ease to know that the rigorous testing process ensures potential risks are minimized. To me the risks pale in comparison to achieving a once-in-a-lifetime opportunity to save someone's life.

I do hope you'll give me a chance to share what I've learned about the recipient's transplant center, their living kidney donor testing process, surgical procedures, recovery timelines and a bit more about who would be receiving my kidney, if I'm able to proceed.

It would mean the world to me to include you in this journey.

[Your signature and contact information below]

Open Letter from a Donor's Mother

I am a mother of a child who donated a kidney to a stranger. At first, I struggled over my daughter's decision. Mothers are supposed to protect their daughters and keep them out of harm's way. I could have benefited greatly from another mother's perspective. In the spirit of empowering other mothers, I wrote this open letter:

Dear Loved One of a Potential Living Kidney Donor:

When my daughter announced she wanted to donate a kidney to a stranger, I was of course concerned. I wasn't as concerned about the surgical outcome as I was for my daughter's future. I thought, "What if she ever had kidney failure herself?" While I've always trusted my daughter's judgment, I couldn't help but ask if she was sure this was something she really wanted to do. She assured us that she had researched the process diligently and that she was 100% confident about her decision.

She expressed her passion for what she believed was a calling to serve. She shared the details of the procedure, highlighting the safeguards that were in place to protect living kidney donors and conveyed the tremendous faith she had in her medical team, which put my mind at ease.

The real turning point for me occurred when I shifted my focus towards my belief in the **Golden Rule**. I simply put myself in the place of the parent with a *child in need* and found my answer.

I asked myself, "How could I stand in the way of my daughter's calling to save someone's life?" I surely wouldn't want someone to stand in the way if *my* child needed such a gift, so how could I stand in the way of another mother's child?

I'm so proud of my daughter and I'm deeply moved by the spirit of her kindness. I'm equally honored to be the mother of such a gifted and selfless soul.

Diane

Thank You Advocates & Potential Donors

Dear (insert advocate's or donor's name)

I'm at a loss of words trying to express how much I appreciate the ways in which you've been supporting my journey. As you know, trying to find a suitable living kidney donor has been an emotional roller-coaster. Yet, thanks to you, the ups and downs of this ride are now filled with hope and great promise.

Whether you're sharing my story, increasing awareness, inspiring future living kidney donors to step forward—or considering this remarkable act of human kindness yourself, I want you to know how deeply touched I am by your kindness.

Because of you, my hope of living a better and longer life appears to be within arm's reach. Because of you, I feel more optimistic about my future and the work I can do (after my transplant) to help others just like me.

I want you to know that the various ways in which you've been helping me advance to transplant have not been overlooked or under-recognized *and* that all your remarkable efforts have meant the world to me.

The world is a better place because of YOU. And, because of YOU, mine already is.

With deep respect and immense gratitude,

_____

*"I donated one of my kidneys
in a Paired Donation Program
to help six donors and six recipients
(including myself and my husband)
bring the hope of transplant
to life!"* Michelle Fulcher

*"I'm not a hero.
I'm a nurse who wanted
to walk my talk and do more.
I donated one of my kidneys to
help an unrelated kindred-spirit.
We matched as close as sisters!"*
Melissa Blevins Bein

*"I donated one of my kidneys
to my children's elementary
school principal. We now share
a very special bond. I continue
to lead an active and amazing
life. Best decision ever!"*
Kati Woelker

Listing at Multiple Transplant Centers

It is possible to list at more than one transplant center if the transplant centers are located in different UNOS regions of the country. This strategy is often considered when seeking shorter wait times. The United States is divided into eleven transplant regions. While multi-listings can be an advantage, certain factors need to be considered. For example, some centers may have longer wait times. Others may not allow multiple listings. Repeat evaluation testing may also be required. Travel time and insurance network coverage can also limit options.

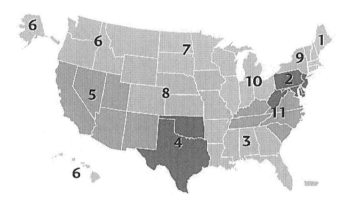

- Region 1: Ct, ME, MA, NH, RI, Eastern VT
- Region 2: DE, DC, MD, NJ, PA, WV, Northern VA
- Region 3: AL, AR, FL, GA, LA, MS, PR
- Region 4: OK, TX
- Region 5: AZ, CA, NV, NM, UT
- Region 6: AK, HI, ID, MT, OR, WA
- Region 7: IL, MN, ND, SD, WI
- Region 8: CO, IA, KS, MO NE, WY
- Region 9: NY, Western VT
- Region 10: IN, MI, OH
- Region 11: KY, NC, SC, TN, VA

Note: *Candidates can transfer wait time by ending their listing at one transplant center and transferring to another, when coordinated.*

Campaign Tracking Spreadsheet

	CONTACT LIST NAMES	EMAIL ADDRESS	SENT BY	LETTER TYPE	DATE SENT	FOLLOW UP ACTION
1						
2						
3						
4						
5						
6						
7						
8						
9						
10						
11						
12						
13						
14						
15						
16						
17						
18						
19						
20						
21						
22						
23						
24						
25						
26						
27						

Scripting My Story - Worksheet

_____

_____

_____

_____

_____

_____

_____

_____

_____

_____

_____

_____

_____

_____

_____

_____

_____

_____

_____

_____

_____

_____

_____

_____

My Intention Statement - Worksheet

_____

_____

_____

_____

_____

_____

_____

_____

_____

_____

_____

_____

_____

_____

_____

_____

_____

_____

_____

_____

_____

_____

_____

_____

_____

_____

_____

_____

My Donor Outreach Team - Worksheet

Social Events & Fundraising - Worksheet

_____

_____

_____

_____

_____

_____

_____

_____

_____

_____

_____

_____

_____

_____

_____

_____

_____

_____

_____

_____

_____

_____

_____

_____

_____

_____

Story Posting Locations - Worksheet

_____

_____

_____

_____

_____

_____

_____

_____

_____

_____

_____

_____

_____

_____

_____

_____

_____

_____

_____

_____

_____

_____

_____

_____

_____

_____

_____

_____

Volunteer Opportunities – Worksheet

Action List & Reminders – Worksheet

_____

_____

_____

_____

_____

_____

_____

_____

_____

_____

_____

_____

_____

_____

_____

_____

_____

_____

_____

_____

_____

_____

_____

_____

Action List & Reminders – Worksheet

_____

_____

_____

_____

_____

_____

_____

_____

_____

_____

_____

_____

_____

_____

_____

_____

_____

_____

_____

_____

_____

_____

_____

_____

_____

REFERENCES

1. Fissel, RB, Srinivas, T, et al. *Preemptive renal transplant candidate survival, Access to Care and Renal Function at Listing.* Oxford Journals NDT.2012.

2. Abramowicz, D Hazzan, M, et al. Does Preemptive Transplantation versus Post Start of Dialysis Transplantation with a Kidney from a Living Donor Improve Outcomes After Transplantation? Oxford Journals NDT.2015.

3. OPTN/SRTR 2010 Annual Data Report. Published in American journal of Transplantation 12:2012 (supplement 1)

4. National Kidney Registry. *Deceased Donor vs. Living Donor Transplants.* http://www.kidneyregistry.org/living_donors.php

5. Beth Israel Deaconess Medical Center. Harvard Medical School Teaching Hospital. *The Benefits of Transplant versus Dialysis;* http://www.bidmc.org/Centers-and Departments/Departments/Transplant-Institute/Kidney/The-Benefits-of-Transplant-versus-Dialysis.aspx

6. Kasiske, B.L, Snyder, Jon. J, Matas, Arthur. J, Ellison, Mary. D, Gill, John S., Kausz, Annamaria T. JASN. *Preemptive Kidney Transplantation: The Advantage and the Advantaged*; 1. 2002

7. Grams, Morgan E. Massie, Allan. B, Segev, Dorry L. *Trends in The Timing of Pre-emptive Kidney Transplantation.* JASN. Sep (9): 1615-1620. 2011

8. WaitList Zero, *Dialysis is not a Long-Term Solution;* http://waitlistzero.org/the-kidney-crisis/

9. National Kidney Foundation. *Religion and Organ Donation.* https://www.kidney.org/atoz/content/Religion-Organ-Donation

10. National Organ Transplantation Act. 1984. https://www.livingdonorassistance.org/documents/NOTA.pdf

11. National Kidney Foundation. *Living Donor Act* https://www.kidney.org/news/national-kidney-foundation-urges-support-living-donor-protection-act

RESOURCES & LINKS

Patient Empowerment, Support & Mentoring

American Transplant Foundation
1+1=LIFE Mentorship Program
600 17th Street, Suite 2515 South
Denver, CO 80202
Email: support@americantransplantfoundation.org
http://www.americantransplantfoundation.org/

National Kidney Foundation Peers Support
For Kidney Patients & Living Donors
30 East 33rd Street
New York, NY 10016
855-653-7337
Email: NKFpeers@kidney.org
Web: https://www.kidney.org/patients/peers

Polycystic Kidney Disease Foundation (PKDF)
Dedicated to finding treatments and a cure for Polycystic Kidney Disease
1001 E. 101st Terrace, Suite 220,
Kansas City, MO, 64131
800.PKD.CURE
Email: pkdcure@pkdcure.org
Web: https://pkdcure.org

Renal Support Network
Patients Helping Patients Peer Support HopeLine
1146 N. Central Ave. #121
Glendale, CA 91207
(800) 579-1970
www.rsnhope.org

TransplantFirst Academy
Empowerment Coaching, Motivational Seminars & Advocacy
10869 N. Scottsdale Rd, Ste 103-537
Scottsdale, AZ 85254
Email: risa@TransplantFirst.org
Web: https://TransplantFirst.org

Statistical Data & Resources

Scientific Registry of Transplant Recipients (SRTR)
Find A Kidney Transplant Center & Calculate Your Wait Time
A Minneapolis Medical Research Foundation
914 S. 8th Street, Minneapolis, MN 55404
877-970-SRTR
www.SRTR.org

United Network for Organ Sharing (UNOS)
Organ Procurement and Transplantation Network
Managed by US Department of Health & Human Services
Health Resources and Services Administration (HRSA)
Post Office Box 2484, Richmond, VA 23218
Web: https://optn.transplant.hrsa.gov/data/

Centers for Medicare and Medicaid Services (CMS)
U.S. Department of Health and Human Services
End State Renal Disease (ESRD) Medicare & Medicaid Information & Benefits
https://www.medicare.gov/people-like-me/esrd/esrd.html

Educational Resources

American Association of Kidney Patients (AAKP)
The Voice of All Kidney Patients for Education & Support
14440 Bruce B. Downs Blvd. Tampa, Florida, 33613
800 749-AAKP
Email: info@ aakp.org
Web: www.aakp.org

American Society of Transplantation (AST)
Supporting transplant research, public health & organ donation
"One Transplant for Life"
1120 Route 73, Suite 200 Mt. Laurel, NJ 08054
Web: http://power2save.org/

Living Kidney Donors Network (LKDN)
Newsletters, Webinars & Workshops,
1001 Green Bay Rd. Suite 178, Winnetka, IL 60093
Web: http://www.lkdn.org/

National Kidney Center (NKC)
Online Kidney Community for Information, Options & Hope
20081 Whistling Straits Place, Ashburn, VA 20147
Web: www.nationalkidneycenter.org

National Kidney Foundation (NKF)
Patient Education, Peer Mentoring & Support
"Big Ask, Big Give"
30 East 33rd Street, New York, NY 10016
800 622 9010
Email: nkfcares@kidney.org
Web: www.kidney.org

Polycystic Kidney Disease Foundation (PKDF)
Dedicated to finding treatments and a cure for Polycystic Kidney Disease
1001 E. 101st Terrace, Suite 220, Kansas City, MO, 64131
800.PKD.CURE
Email: pkdcure@pkdcure.org
Web: https://pkdcure.org

Reach Kidney Care
Real Engagement Achieving Complete Health
2010 Church Street, Ste 506, Nashville, TN 37203
615-649-0620
Email: christa.lawson@reachkidneycare.org
https://www.reachkidneycare.org

The Proactive Path
Kidney Patient Mentoring, Coaching, Seminars & Books
10869 N. Scottsdale Rd, Ste 103-537, Scottsdale, AZ 85254
480 575 9353
Email: Risa@TheProactivePath.com
Web: www.TheProactivePath.com

The Living Bank
Advancing Living Donation to Confront Needed Organs
PO Box 6725, 4545 Post Oak Place Drive #340, Houston, TX 77027
800-528-2971
Email: info@livingbank.org
Web: www.livingbank.org

TransplantFirst Academy (TFA)
Motivational Seminars, Webinars, Role-Play Videos & Books
10869 N. Scottsdale Rd, Ste 103-537, Scottsdale, AZ 85254
480 575 9353
Email: Risa@TransplantFirst.org
Web: www.TransplantFirst.org

Awareness Campaigns & Financial Resources

American Living Organ Donor Network *(Also known as: ALODF)*
A Project of the Center for Ethical Solutions
Providing financial assistance for non-medical donation related expenses, including lost wages, up to $10,000.
40357 Featherbed Lane, Lovettsville VA 20180.
Email: info@helplivingdonorssavelives.org
Web: http://www.helplivingdonorssavelives.org/

National Living Donor Assistance Center (NLDAC)
Provides limited financial reimbursement assistance for travel and subsistence expenses for donor evaluations and surgery.
2461 S Clark Street, Suite 640, Arlington, VA 22202
888.870.5002
Web: https://www.livingdonorassistance.org
Screening Eligibility Tool:
https://www.livingdonorassistance.org/documents/Eligibility_Screening_Tool.pdf

Paired-Donation Programs

The National Kidney Registry
The nation's most active *Kidney Paired Donation* program. Record-breaking number of paired exchanges completed in a one month's time; a total of fifty paired exchange transplants were completed through NKR in July 2016.
P.O Box 460, Babylon, NY 11702
800 401-8919
www.kidneyregistry.org

Alliance for Paired Donation
In 2004, transplant surgeon Dr. Michael Rees (with the help of his father, computer programmer Alan Rees), performed his first transplant using this platform and first prototype for paired kidney donation matching.
PO Box 965, Perrysburg, OH 43552
877-APKD4ALL
admin@paireddonation.org
www.paireddonation.org

United Network for Organ Sharing/Paired Donation (UNOS)
700 N. 4th Street, Richmond, VA 23219
(804) 782-4800
https://www.unos.org/donation/kidney-paired-donation/

About the Author

The highlight of **Risa Simon's** life was the day an unexpected, unrelated, living kidney donor offered to give her a kidney *and* tests revealed a sister-like match. That day didn't come easy — and it might never have, if she wasn't willing to become a proactive contender, competing for her best life possible.

Risa knows all too well what it's like to be a kidney patient trapped in a hopeless sinkhole headed towards dialysis. As she watched her renal function numbers decline, her emotions escalated. The thought of surrendering her sense of control started to immobilize her future dreams. Something she wasn't willing to give up so easily.

When she pulled back the curtain and took a deeper dive, she discovered a hidden paradigm that compelled her to stand before her disease. She began to use her voice to empower a superior choice—a transplant *before* the need for dialysis.

Today, Risa is living her best life ever as a preemptive (live-donor) transplant recipient. Known as a pioneer and "positive-disruptor," Risa traded in 3 decades of practice management consulting success to create a better tomorrow for her fellow kidney patients.

Risa's passion for patient engagement reflects in the names of her firms, *The Proactive Path* and the *TransplantFirst Academy*.

Best known for her motivational seminars, inspirational mentoring, thought-provoking webinars, patient advocacy and trailblazing empowerment books, Risa invites her fans and followers to "join her at the top" – where dreams can come true.

Books Written by this Author

Shift Your Fate: Life-Changing Wisdom for Proactive Kidney Patients

If you've been diagnosed with kidney disease and feel like you've lost control over your future, or you've been told "there's nothing you can do until your renal function plummets" – listen up! You can do something—and the time is now.

This book takes its readers on a journey that begins with the importance of proactive self-advocacy. Unspoken facts that differentiate dialysis and transplant are revealed to help kidney patients use their voice to optimize choice.

If you seek a stronger partnership with your doctors and want to influence your destiny by becoming a fierce advocate for a live-donor kidney transplant, this book is the place to begin.

(Published 2012. Revised July 2016)

In Pursuit of a Better Life: The Ultimate Guide for Finding Living Kidney Donors

The thought of having to find someone willing to donate one of their kidneys can be undeniably overwhelming. The challenge only intensifies when candidates aren't provided instructional guidance on how to go about the process.

This book was written to bridge the information gap—by empowering dialogues, expanding outreach and boosting the possibility of good fortune. Readers will be armed with advanced living donor communication skills, template letters and proactive strategies to increase need awareness and attract potential donors.

Early adopters will discover their **Donor-Magnet® superpowers** by enlisting an army of spokespersons to serve on a dedicated **Donor Outreach Team**—charged with helping them reach their goals.

(Released January 2017. Enhanced November 2017)

TRANSPLANTFIRST
EMPOWERED PATIENT ACADEMY

The TransplantFirst Academy (TFA) is a 501c3 non-profit corporation that exists to ensure all eligible kidney patients are given an opportunity to proactively pursue a preemptive path to a (live-donor) transplant *before* they approach the need for dialysis.

TFA educates transplant candidates, including transplant-eligible dialysis patients, on living kidney donor communication strategies that offer a faster track to transplant.

TFA passionately advocates for initiatives that recognize and protect living kidney donors for saving and improving lives— and inspiring ordinary people to seek extraordinary acts of human kindness.

Website: TransplantFirst.org

Email: Risa@TransplantFirst.org

Seminars, Webinars:
Mentoring & Coaching Risa@TheProactivePath.com

Book Website: FindingKidneyDonors.com

Book Orders: Available on Amazon

Made in the USA
Middletown, DE
29 September 2019